D0782954

Songs for Dead Children

Songs for Dead Children

E.D. Blodgett

 THE UNIVERSITY OF ALBERTA PRESS

Published by

THE UNIVERSITY OF ALBERTA PRESS
Ring House 2
Edmonton, Alberta, Canada T6G 2E1
www.uap.ualberta.ca

Copyright © 2018 E.D. Blodgett

LIBRARY AND ARCHIVES CANADA CATALOGUING IN PUBLICATION

Blodgett, E.D. (Edward Dickinson), 1935–, author
    Songs for dead children / E.D. Blodgett.

(Robert Kroetsch Series)
Poems.
Issued in print and electronic formats.
ISBN 978-1-77212-369-2 (softcover).—ISBN 978-1-77212-388-3 (EPUB).—
ISBN 978-1-77212-387-6 (Kindle).—ISBN 978-1-77212-386-9 (PDF)

    1. Mahler, Gustav, 1860–1911. Kindertotenlieder—Poems.
I. Title. II. Series: Robert Kroetsch series

PS8553.L56S66 2018   C811'.54 C2017-906793-1
                          C2017-906794-X

First edition, first printing, 2018.
First printed and bound in Canada by Houghton Boston Printers,
    Saskatoon, Saskatchewan.
Copyediting and proofreading by Peter Midgley.

A volume in the Robert Kroetsch Series.

All rights reserved. No part of this publication may be produced, stored in
a retrieval system, or transmitted in any form or by any means (electronic,
mechanical, photocopying, recording, or otherwise) without prior written
consent. Contact the University of Alberta Press for further details.

The University of Alberta Press supports copyright. Copyright fuels
creativity, encourages diverse voices, promotes free speech, and creates a
vibrant culture. Thank you for buying an authorized edition of this book
and for complying with the copyright laws by not reproducing, scanning,
or distributing any part of it in any form without permission. You are
supporting writers and allowing the University of Alberta Press to continue
to publish books for every reader.

The University of Alberta Press is committed to protecting our natural
environment. As part of our efforts, this book is printed on Enviro Paper: it
contains 100% post-consumer recycled fibres and is acid- and chlorine-free.

The University of Alberta Press gratefully acknowledges the support
received for its publishing program from the Government of Canada, the
Canada Council for the Arts, and the Government of Alberta through the
Alberta Media Fund.

infantibus mortuis et vivis

et tibi

Oft denk' ich, sie sind nur ausgegangen,

Bald werden sie wieder nach Hause gelangen.

[Often I think they just stepped out to play

And soon they will be home again to stay.]

—Friedrich Rückert, Gustave Mahler:

Kindertotenlieder IV

1

Everyone stands alone on the heart of the earth

long beneath the darkening skies
they play

running down the long paths
lined with cherry trees
and strange flowers

the dust not dust beneath their feet
but flecks of pale gold
tossed into the air

lie down lie down
what hidden god cries out
and all

among the pastures spread out
beside the rolling hills
lie down

their only thought
to be green
to be the green pastures

to be
the clean innocence of green

alone

a solitude
that lies open between
you

and the first star
of nothing and
spatial dust

your hands reaching
deeply into all
the nothing around you

you
the first star
the barest light

the loneliness that you reflect
curling into your heart

immeasurable all
the silence that
rises in your eyes

no one can tell the origin
of what was heard

or if it came in words
but all the air commanded it

lie down
embrace the earth

almost disappearing into grass
and every smaller cry and sound

flesh alone knows
the words that stones speak

it was
nothing that
had been exhaled

clouds that lift beyond
the reach of small hands
nothing that

passing leaves
nothing in its wake but sky

or lies
unshaken on a pond
nothing to grasp

but water
flowing away

nothing that
lies so lightly on your eyes

grace embodied
in certain ways of walking
a slow dance that

wherever it goes
it moves unerringly
the music that it makes

rising in small leaps

heaven is not
a final move
heaven is

the flow we see
as bodies changing shape
the flow that carries the heart

into the world

as one
lying alone in bed

suddenly seeing the first snow
the first that he remembers

snow that does not fall
but randomly appears
from somewhere in the dark air

a snow that is
seen at once in the mind
snow that has come forever

and then
lilacs unbidden
appeared

standing in the mind
the power of their fragrance
purple and white

a memory of lilacs that
displaced all that might
have been

what child now
stands beside them overcome

and which
more immortal
lilac or child

awake
only to gaze upon the moon

riding unperturbed
upon the eye

nothing that can
be held
and nothing

that is not possessed
by the whole moon

the huge seas
forests transfixed
silence always transformed

how small we are
the merest pebble
overwhelming each of us

over the low wall
and down the slope above the lake

the pears slowly hung
and all the valleys slept

on such a day
your mouth opened
and from it music fell

on such a day
you learned the word untaught
for God

standing apart
along the river's edge
a heron as if

cut from a book
of royal birds appeared

no bird
was standing there
but all his mystery

all day you tried
to put it on
as if mystery were a dress

as if in him
all that was eternity
were not asleep

acrobats
of unbridled suns

gravity
holds no fears for them

rising and falling
as small fountains fall

with them
immortality is born

stars unseen
before their dance begins

strolling under parasols
beneath the summer sun
poppies passing your eyes

the plain magnificence of bees
stirring the air across the field
no other sound but theirs

and one lark that sings out of sight
lifting everything beneath
higher toward a sky you almost touch

strollers have
nowhere they must go
their one desire the moment when

they pass
the sun and all bees
sleeping in their small hands

when you were first
taken to the sea

you fell down upon your knees
and wept

unable to grasp
eternity

invisible
your knees bear still
signs of your falling down

and moving over you
tides that have become
the way you walk

stepping with care
as one struck blind

given to see
and not to see

hidden in the map you held
dragons breathed
perhaps in the woods
perhaps behind the hills

your eyes followed the stream
a line that disappeared
somewhere in the woods
where a spring rises

who are you
lost beside the stream
and where have you gone
wandered into trees

if you are known to birds
by what name are you called
where smoke rises from a house
are you drawn home

the sun never sets
behind the trees
eternity
held in your hands

a bird stands on your heart
waiting for dusk

all other birds
grown silent

and echoing their song
music like a slow rain

flows upon your flesh
the small bowl of hands

your first desire was
to be snow

not the eternal fall of snow
but the first

the day you saw the air
transformed into

petals falling from
acacia trees

the white breath of being
exhaling again

all the animals went by
without a name

one crossed the moon
its shadow cast upon your skin

a dry gentle rain it was
that never went away

others fly near
no more afraid of you
than of the moon

as bells that ring through
the winter air

the clear laughter of children
sings in the trees

almost like brooks
bursting in spring

the air stands up
its joy unbound

the breath of it
the bright birth of stars

to be a bird
to feel feathers spring in your skin
to leap up

and never to fall
the air bathing your face
flying over the sea

given to the great wheel
of the turning year
and sun everlasting

your blood the long halloo
of gladness carrying your heart
into the light

time that kept you paused
and like a flower rose into the air

where to lay your broken doll
but on the sill of all things
that are without time

knowing that
beside it you were to pray

not in words
but in the measure of
waves that fall upon a shore

learning how
to practise immortality

as if you were to take
music into your hands
rocking it to sleep

2

pierced through by a ray of sun

who can bear
the loneliness of dogs

sitting beside
the small plots of graves

barking softly
marking the hours of night

as one who walks and walks
through high water
moving without moving

hardly to be seen
on the edge of a road
her palms held up

as one who bears
an offering
for no god in sight

and over her arms
a ragged dress
with no body inside

walking and walking
along the ends of the earth

when you lost them all
your breath turned black
exhaling night

the moaning that you heard
was night alone
that moaned

no mother now
to lift you out of darkness
no wings to be yours

were you to pray
the words that fall from your mouth
would make the sound
of small stones at prayer

she could not walk
without making little hops
and so she passed

over logs
across mud
through lengths of stony fields

she learned that walking was
a way of dancing
through the sun

when soldiers came
she failed to see them there
and how they fired on all that moved

who shall dare to wash
the lovely feet of them that pass
over the highest mountains

so little left behind
no more than can be placed
in two small hands

the last to see him was the sun
and the first

his head at rest
upon the stony ground
no one to stroke his hair

no one was heard
bidding him farewell

the wholeness of the world
broken in the wind
the cries of birds dispersed

so little
left behind

across the plain
the sad donkeys walk

bearing the deaths of children
in their mournful eyes

what is there
to understand

all have been taken away
by water fire and falling rocks

dancing into death
borne across the mourning plains

too swift to stay
he turned and disappeared

no bird
slipping into a hedge
with such speed

the briefest absence of being
standing where he stood

a broken pair of shoes
no other sign left behind
that he had been

against the moon
invisible breaths of dust

hunters walk against
a sky of porcelain blue
shooting doves

one after another

so was she
found alone against the sky

to fall like them
the lovely axis of the world
bleeding across a sky

of porcelain blue

beautiful
so beautiful the eyes

gazing up at the world

clouds passing over them
pause in the waning light

birds turn slowly
unable to depart

silence rises from stones
shaping all the music

no one hears

so beautiful the eyes
their light spent

never to grow old
to sit beside the sea
to gaze at the shape of clouds

to have a memory of things
simply to love the sun

never to know a past
that would become what he was
a way of seeing trees

to gather the shadows
of long afternoons

never to learn grace
never to consume
the whole of the autumn moon

the birds he burned to be
flew in zigzags
above the spot
where he went up

a place of stone and ash

above the birds
the empty air
crazed with small cries
thin as sticks

broken urn of fire

how many herons stand
around the bay

watching over them
who vanished here

the water of the world
lies on their backs

the silence they keep
deeper than the bay

where her heart had stood
the stars turn slowly

birds who come and go
gaze at each one
before departing

no other light
known to them

her darkness
the emptiness that cradles the sun

over the water
where calmly asleep they lie
all the willows weep

or was it long strands of hair
that weep in deep silence there

as music departs
leaving silence in its wake

she had a way
of walking out of a room
and leaving silence behind

but when the earth
was blown apart
she entered it

taking the music she was
and all the silence of the world

as old men do
he will not sit beside the sea
his mind filled with thoughts

his quick death
his small parcel of bones
will not be known to him

he gazes only into a dream
that bears no mortality
holding him in deepest sleep

gazing into the word
he will become

a naked word
barely coming to mind

like paper dolls stepping on
a blue horizon
they make their way

keeping their balance
by the way they sing
back and forth

and hunters in their happiness
pick them off one by one
as at a country fair

without a sound
they slip unnoticed into the earth
leaving it unscathed

she had a voice
that when she sang
resembled the break of day

the light that gave
the world its shape
and made the stones dance

and when she sang
innocence
itself began to sing

one day her voice
no longer sang
and silence fell from the sky

the sun fell
and she fell
the curtain of air fell

the stones sang
the grass sang
their silence without echo

like nothing else
no metaphor can grasp
his coming and his going away

but so complete inside himself
it seemed that there were things
that resembled him

as one might say
the sun appeared like he appeared
his radiance unfailing

or the moon
as he was seen but partially
clouds moving past

and in his absence
what can be said of the sun
no one needs the moon

enclosed in his death
all signs of how he might have been
scattered in the wind

and so she
stepped through a gate
never to be seen again

only her small pile of bones
scraps of her dress
her lovely hair

her soul on fire
stepped forth
to greet her brother sun

her hands
or where her hands had been
spilling over in fountains of light

3

and suddenly it's evening

a slow evening it was
in June

when the sun stopped
not brought to an end

but pausing just enough
to divide the light

from darkness
and there between them both you stood

a bell ringing
softly through the dark

a bell
ringing over quiet waters

as bands of rain that fall
across a vast savannah
rain and then bursts

of sunlight lilting back and forth

so the world opens
almost at your feet
the world simply at play

children are
the only creatures visible
and all of them

leaping and dancing through
the showers of rain
leaping and dancing without fear

as if a god of play
was risen from the earth to hold
the sun and rain

and children leaping and dancing

the only sound
springs of laughter playing
like water rippling over stones

almost never
do their feet touch the ground
barely brushing the grass

shadows slowly
of intricate pavanes
like steps of birds along a shore

fall here and there behind

as if the frail memories
of whom they may have been
float down upon the ground

and sleep

infinities of bees
singing jubilate
through the silence that

flowers keep

and into this
soft communion she
unthinking steps

walking into the space
possessed by joy
as one might fall

into a language never heard

translated into
the tongue of bees
to be how joy would be

and water
remembered as
a fountain in the mind

splashing over him
as if he had been
a mountain behind clouds

his being
falling water all
the being that is

now you are
given to remember things
you never knew before

the music of the moon
settling over
night-flying birds

the seas that sing through
invisible stratospheres
of breeching whales

o memory the pure
light without beginning
singing through all breathing things

the singing trees and grass
the keening arias of the wind
giving breath to bright stones

an eternal now
of crystalline transparency
poised over still waters

a now
of rock and reed and branch
and unmoving moon

a child on the shore
and all at rest upon
the surface of her eye

spare axis of light
holding night and day
in one now of one breath

in him the sea
unfolds in perfect calm

all that it has
all its comings and goings
surrendered gladly to the moon

and he
follows the lines it spreads
sinuously through his heart

and all the wheeling birds of the sea
align with him
his heart their moon

things that come
nearest to eternity

trees and stones and stars

live by silence
their sole breath

and when she stands
beneath the silent trees
she hears them breathe

and breathing in reply
their breath flowing through itself
so they speak

she and all trees
praising the one breath
before the trees were breathed

the moon taking shape

their one reason
is the sun

when they speak
it is the sun
that stands upon their tongues

and when they play
it is light and fire
surrounding them

and through the great day
they turn with slow magnificence
attending the moon

the dreams they have
the rising of the stars

but to play
the only way to reach
the other

playing gods

all dancing on the shore
tracks of their feet
impressed on sand

and dancing over them
the feet of children
enmeshed

almost to be
a god

quick ballets that fall
between the water and the shore
a dance that flows

following the breathing moon

around their heads
wreaths of smoke
gilded by the sun

walking down
the endless boulevards
haloed under trees

stones at their feet
invisible
and clouds of sleeping rain

enchanted the moon
glides on heaven
and on their golden tongues

like early spring rain
light grazes over her face

that lifts toward its passing
as swallows lift and fall

the air and their
barely moving wings
in one stroke

of lifting and falling away

all of her
a breathing in
and breathing out of light

the deeper light flowing forth
as if a single breath
had swept through her

and the waiting sun

poplar leaves
on windless summer afternoons
whisper among themselves

speaking of the wind and leaves
as if they were
children of the sun

whose voices tune
to speak as lazy rivers might
or stones answering the sun

their voices rising from
a light invisible
their breath the breath

of grass springing from the ground

the slightest step across grass
and echoes of smaller feet
spring up among

the leaves and stillest stones

what music is this
so random no one can
find its replica

the ghosts of children will
never reveal themselves
infinitesimal music all

they can yield up

sudden rustles of
swift departures
their being what they were

what moves her to stand
when evening settles through the air
beside a pond

to gaze slowly at the water
beside the reeds and small rocks
waiting for her to come

to see herself there

floating at her feet
broken slightly by the waves
covered by a watery moon

reeds rising through her hands

birds dip over her
the breeze lifting this small
and infinite being without name

what moves her if not
the quiet reeds within her
the floating moon

birds shedding their light shade

without waiting for
the coming of dark
stars hold their place

beyond all darkness
saving the light
where their stars emerge

burning through their hearts
to rest unfailing on
the firmament possessing them

the darkness that surrounds them
invisible against their light
all the being that they are

rising in their eyes
the quick cosmos washed
in light from the first stars

the fire of their breath
enters the smallest stone
and all forgotten things

nothing that does not hold
a certain semblance of the sun
the unswerving clarity of stars

how the autumnal trees
lift up the sun
the fire of it surging through their leaves

beneath them they play
their small steps
dancing round the trees

fire leaping from their hearts
and through the radiant leaves
slow auroras unfolding

through air without time
the ripple of crystal bells

and intricate laughter
falling through afternoons

with the deep pace of lotus petals
that open to the late air

keeping the ritual
of laughter and the bells

the lotus suspended on
the ecstasies of water

and where they walk
stillness like morning dew
settles upon them

both ground and feet
meeting in blessings of
bliss ineffable

every step they take
a ceremony of the trees
standing through their seasons

the breath of their leaves
reaching slowly to the stars
in verdant hallelujahs

Acknowledgements

The title of this book is taken from Gustave Mahler's
Kindertotenlieder, a song cycle based on five poems
from a series of poems by Friedrich Rückert.

The epigraphs are my translation from Salvatore
Quasimodo's epigram, "Ed è subito sera":

Everyone stands alone on the heart of the earth
pierced through by a ray of sun
and suddenly it's evening.

Other Titles from The University of Alberta Press

Elegy

E.D. Blodgett

A lament in light. A breath-taking memorial.
Poetry and photography that compose the
landscapes of remembrance.

cuRRents Series

as if

E.D. Blodgett

A poet's visceral musings explore the
intertwining connection between the
human and the natural worlds.

Robert Kroetsch Series

An Ark of Koans

E.D. Blodgett

A meditation on the mystery of what
happens at the moment it happens.

cuRRents Series

More information at www.uap.ualberta.ca